INVINCIBLE INTRODUCTION
by Tom Brevoort

The first time I met Robert Kirkman in person, he insulted my shoes. He sat right there, in a guest chair in my office up at Marvel and just leaned over and insulted my shoes. Now, as a general rule, this isn't the best way to endear yourself to an editor to whom you intend to sell yourself as a prospective writer. I certainly don't endorse it as a game plan. And yet, Robert ended up working on CAPTAIN AMERICA for me, and MARVEL TEAM-UP, and MARVEL KNIGHTS 2099, and probably a couple more things by the time you read this introduction.

The reason for this shocking turn of events, as unbelievable as any twist ending he ever wrote into a comic book tale, can be found within the stories contained within this third volume of INVINCIBLE, the superhero strip Kirkman co-created with Cory Walker, who himself owes me some pages at the moment.

INVINCIBLE unabashedly showcases the author's love of the superhero genre—all of its color, its vibrancy, and even its silliness. It's a comic book that isn't ashamed of being a comic book—and that's what attracted me to it when one of the dozens of copies of the first INVINCIBLE trade paperback that Kirkman had been flooding the Marvel offices witch fell into my hands.

INVINCIBLE is fun. Or, at least it was up till now.

The stories in this volume of INVINCIBLE transition the title between the way-it-had-been into the series it was meant to become. Such "everything-you-know-is-wrong" tales have been a staple of the industry since Alan Moore pretty much popularized them in the early 1980s. The difference here is that it's no Johnny-come-lately overturning the apple carts that make the series work, no latter-day genius stretching for the twist that'd reinvigorate interest in a long-running franchise. This turn of events was part of the original series conception right from the get-go—or at least that's what Kirkman maintains, but with that guy, who can really tell.

In any case, the good news is that, even with the startling reversals that await you on the coming pages, INVINCIBLE has lost none of its sparkle, none of its wit and none of its charm. If anything, these stories turned the dial up to eleven, increasing the drama and the tension in the tradition of the best superhero soap operas that preceded it.

Robert himself wears slip-on sneakers, which contain an elastic fastener that expands to allow one's foot to be inserted. This in marked contrast to my own Velcro-fastened sneakers. So far as I know, he never commented on the footwear of either Brian Michael Bendis or Kurt Busiek, which might explain the good words they had for his work when the subject came up. Or maybe they were just trying to disguise their own tardiness with deadlines by distracting a frazzled editor. Whatever the reason, it worked.

As it seems to have worked on the industry in general. And so, we've watched this boy wonder conquer the world of comicdom, one series at a time, one reader at a time. I swear, he's writing something like a third of the items listed in the monthly Diamond Previews catalogue at this point. And he's been nominated for an Eisner award, which he deserves at the very least for his productivity. But the best, I think, is yet to come, as the added exposure of his upcoming gigs is sure to make Kirkman's name a household word in comic book buying households coast to coast.

And along the way Robert invited me to write the introduction to the next INVINCIBLE trade paperback. Which was probably meant to seem like sucking up to the boss. But I've been around the business long enough to realize that what Kirkman was really after was somebody he could sucker into pounding out a few hundred words extolling his virtues for free, on their own time—thinking it a compliment. But I did it nonetheless, which casts some questions upon my judgment. Which just goes to show, if you have enough talent, you can get away with anything.

I still maintain they were very nice shoes.

Tom Brevoort

CHAPTER ONE

WHAT IS OUR STATUS, DOWNLOAD?

WE WILL BE VAPORIZED ON THE SURFACE OF THE STAR IN LESS THAN SIX MINUTES.

ENGINEERING. HOW LONG UNTIL THE ENGINES ARE REPAIRED?

THE TERRELIANS DID A NUMBER ON US BEFORE WE GOT THEM, CAPTAIN. IT'S GOING TO TAKE AT *LEAST* FORTY-FIVE MINUTES UNTIL WE'RE BACK ON-LINE.

DAMN IT! WE DON'T HAVE THAT KIND OF TIME!

SIR, IF I CAN CONFIGURE THE DEFLECTOR ARRAY TO EMIT *MULTIPLE* TRACTOR BEAMS IT *MAY* BE POSSIBLE TO SLINGSHOT OURSELVES AWAY FROM THE STAR BY USING THE FRAGMENTED REMAINS OF THE TERRELIAN VESSEL.

MAKE IT S--

DOOM!

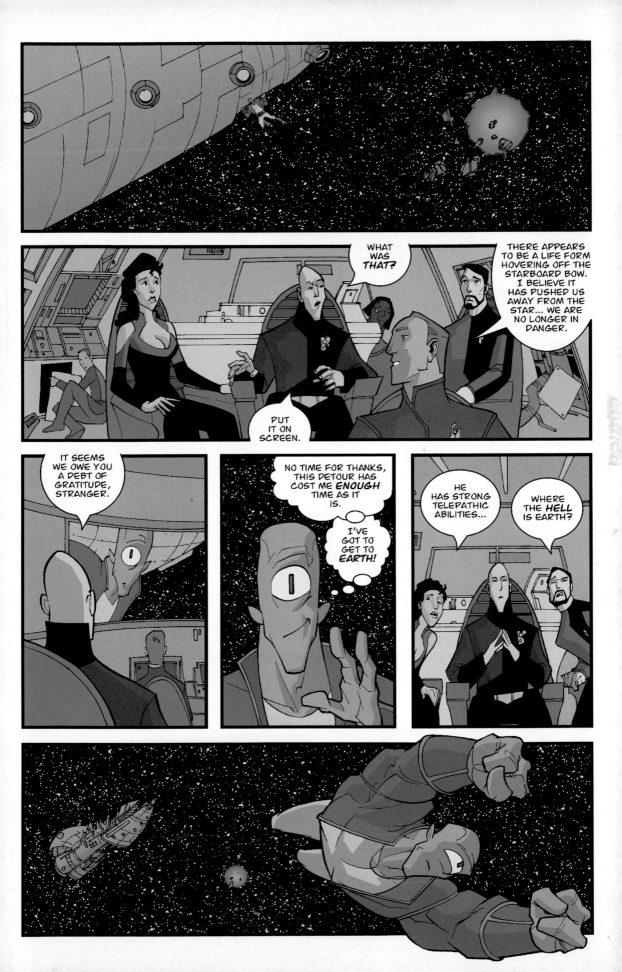

I'LL **ASSUME** YOU'RE WONDERING WHY YOU'RE HERE... FROM WHAT I'VE HEARD ABOUT YOU... YOU MIGHT HAVE ALREADY FIGURED IT OUT.

SIMPLY PUT, YOU WERE A **SHOE-IN**... AND NOW WE'D LIKE **YOU** TO BE IN CHARGE OF FORMING A NEW TEAM THAT **YOU** WILL LEAD.

AS YOU KNOW, THE GUARDIANS OF THE GLOBE WERE RECENTLY AND MYSTERIOUSLY **MURDERED.** AT THE TIME OF THEIR DEATH YOU WERE BEING CONSIDERED AS AN **ADDITION** TO THE TEAM. THE OLD TEAM WORKED **CLOSELY** WITH US, BUT IT WAS A **PRIVATE** ORGANIZATION FUNDED JOINTLY BY DARKWING'S ALTER EGO AND WAR WOMAN. SADLY THERE IS NO ONE THERE TO PICK UP THE TORCH. SO THE GOVERNMENT HAS BEEN **INVITED** TO TAKE OVER.

I AM HONORED THAT YOU HAVE SUCH CONFIDENCE IN MY ABILITIES.

I WILL **NOT** DISAPPOINT YOU.

WE PLAN ON HOLDING A RECRUITMENT MEETING IN THE NEXT FEW DAYS. IF YOU CAN PROVIDE ME WITH A **LIST** OF ANYONE **YOU'D** PREFER TO WORK WITH, I'LL MAKE SURE WE CONTACT THEM.

THAT'S ALL I ASK. NOW, BEHIND ME HERE IS **DONALD**, HE'S OUR SUPER-HUMAN LIAISON. HE'LL BE YOUR CONTACT WITHIN THE GOVERNMENT. YOU'LL ONLY HAVE TO DEAL WITH ME IF SOMETHING GOES **HORRIBLY** WRONG.

PRAY WE **NEVER** MEET AGAIN.

SON... WE NEED TO **TALK.**

≥SIGH≤

MARK, WE NEED TO TALK.

≥SIGH≤

MARK, IT IS **VERY** IMPORTANT THAT WE--

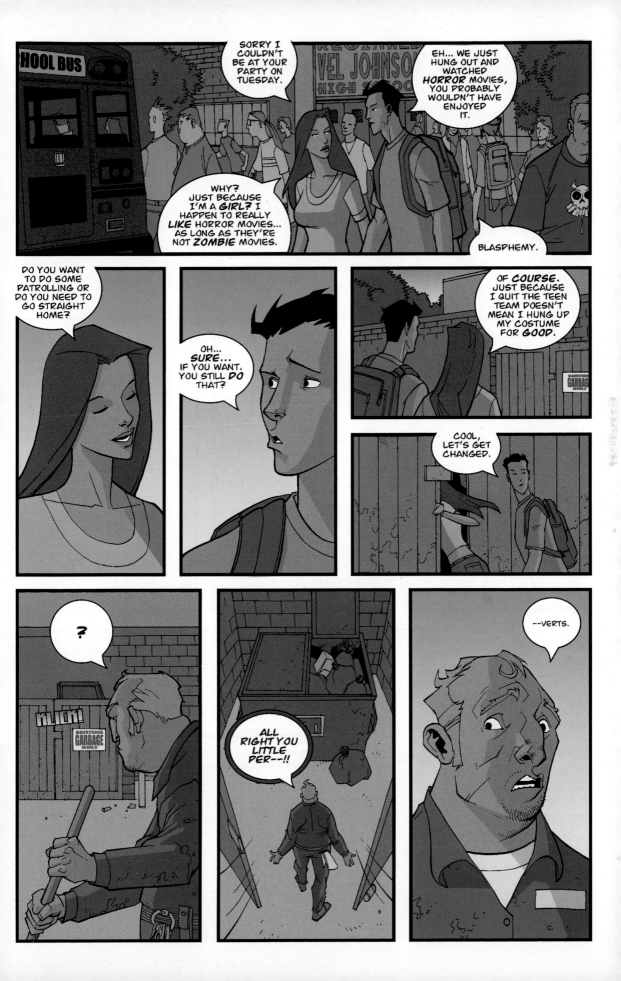

JEEZ.

YEAH, ARE WE ON A SECURE LINE? SORRY TO BOTHER YOU IN THE MIDDLE OF THE DAY BUT MARK *FINALLY* PUT ANOTHER ONE OF HIS COSTUMES IN THE WASH AND I CAN'T REMEMBER IF IT'S COLD THEN *WARM* OR WARM THEN *COLD*. YOU'D THINK I WOULD *KNOW* THIS BUT NOLAN HAS BEEN CLEANING HIS UNIFORMS WITH SOLAR RADIATION SINCE I SHRANK HIS *FIRST* ONE ON ACCIDENT.

IT'S ACTUALLY *COLD* THEN *COLD*, LIKE A COLORFUL SWEATER, BUT YOU SHOULD *REALLY* TALK NOLAN INTO GETTING ONE OF MY *IONIC* CLEANSING MACHINES. IT'D *SURE* SAVE YOU A *LOT* OF WORK.

OH, SILLY ME... I REMEMBER THAT, NOW! AND I'VE *GIVEN UP* ON THE *ION* THING. NOLAN DOESN'T SEEM TO *WORRY* ABOUT GIVING ME MORE READING TIME... AND WE'RE TRYING TO SAVE FOR MARK'S *COLLEGE*.

THANKS FOR THE HELP.

KLIK!

♪

WOW... YOU GUYS GOT *QUITE* THE TURNOUT.

WE'RE GOING TO BE PAYING WELL AND APPARENTLY WORD SPREADS *FAST* IN OUR CIRCLE.

THE *CAPES, INC.* CREW OUT OF NEW YORK ACCOUNTS FOR *HALF* OUR ATTENDANCE... THOSE GUYS ARE *VULTURES.*

REX.

INVINCIBLE.

YOU SHOULDN'T LET HIS ACTIONS TOWARDS *EVE* AFFECT *YOUR* OPINION OF HIM.

I JUST CAN'T *BELIEVE* HE *DID* THAT TO HER.

I CAN'T BELIEVE A *LOT* OF WHAT YOU PEOPLE DO, BUT I TRY NOT TO HOLD IT *AGAINST* YOU.

VERY FUNNY... YOU KNOW *YOU'RE* THE CLONE. I HAD YOU *GET* THE PIERCINGS SO PEOPLE COULD TELL US *APART*.

KEEP TELLING YOURSELF THAT. *I* GOT THESE PIERCINGS TO *DIFFERENTIATE* MYSELF FROM YOU... MY *CLONE*.

YOU WERE THE ORIGINAL AND YOU ALTERED YOUR APPEARANCE AND LET THE *CLONE* KEEP *YOUR* NORMAL LOOK? DOES THAT MAKE ANY SENSE TO YOU?

CONDEMNED. NO TRESPASSING.

OH, *WHATEVER.* BELIEVE WHAT YOU WANT... I *TIRE* OF THIS SUBJECT.

HOW MUCH *MORE* TINKERING MUST YOU DO? I'M *TIRED* OF ALL THIS WAITING.

YOU WANT HIM TO WAKE UP AND *KILL* US? I HAVE TO MAKE SURE THE CONTROL BEACONS ARE OPERATIONAL BEFORE I LOCK DOWN THE SEALS ON THE COLLAR.

IF HE WAKES UP AND HE'S *NOT* UNDER OUR CONTROL WE WILL HAVE SUCCEEDED ONLY IN RESURRECTING ONE OF OUR *WORST* ENEMIES. I TRUST YOU *DON'T* WANT THAT.

JUST *HURRY.*

THERE... STAND BACK I'M GOING TO SEAL IT. ONCE THE CONNECTION IS MADE, HE SHOULD REVIVE *INSTANTLY.*

?

CHAPTER TWO

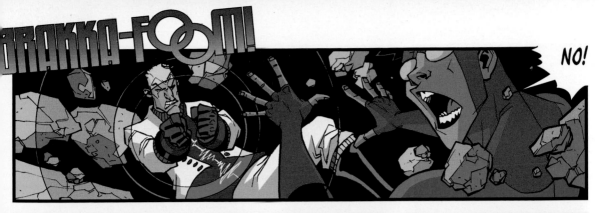

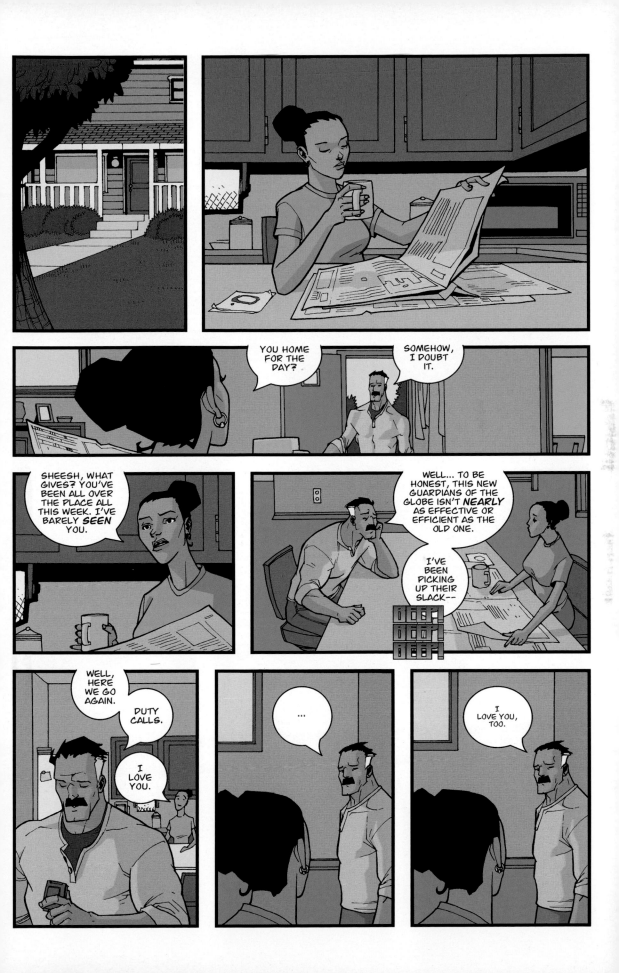

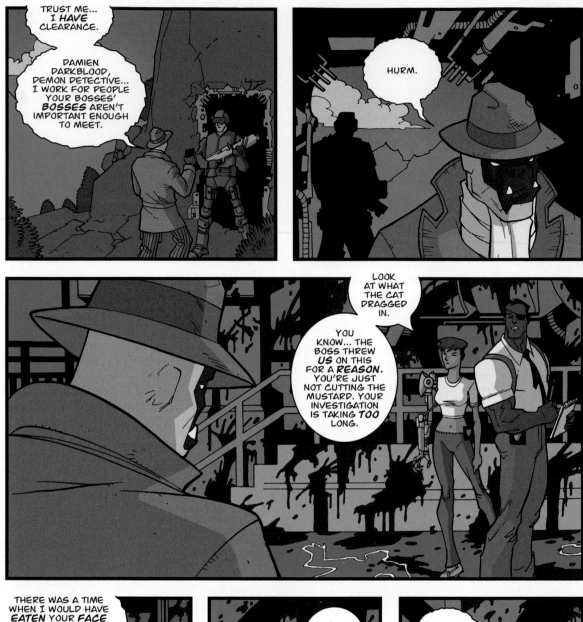

HE'S RIGHT UP HERE. STAY BACK AWAY FROM THE GLASS.

SURE.

SANFORD?

I'LL LEAVE YOU TWO ALONE.

IT FITS YOU WELL, THE COSTUME. I HOPE I DIDN'T *DAMAGE* IT IN MY LITTLE... ESCAPADE.

OH, SANFORD... I WISH YOU HADN'T *DONE* THIS TO YOURSELF.

I DID IT ALL FOR *YOU*, SIR. I COULDN'T *BEAR* ANOTHER GLIMPSE OF WHAT THEY TURNED YOU INTO. I WOULD HAVE KILLED EVERY ONE OF THEM HAD THEY NOT *ALREADY* BEEN DEAD.

STILL... THEY *ARE* DEAD... SO I'VE REALLY GOT *NOTHING* TO COMPLAIN ABOUT.

I'M PART OF THE *NEW* GUARDIANS OF THE GLOBE... I'VE GOT SOME INFLUENCE. I'M DOING WHAT I CAN TO GET YOU *OUT* OF HERE. YOU NEED COUNSELING... NOT INCARCERATION.

I WOULD *CERTAINLY* WELCOME THE CHANCE TO LEAVE THIS PLACE.

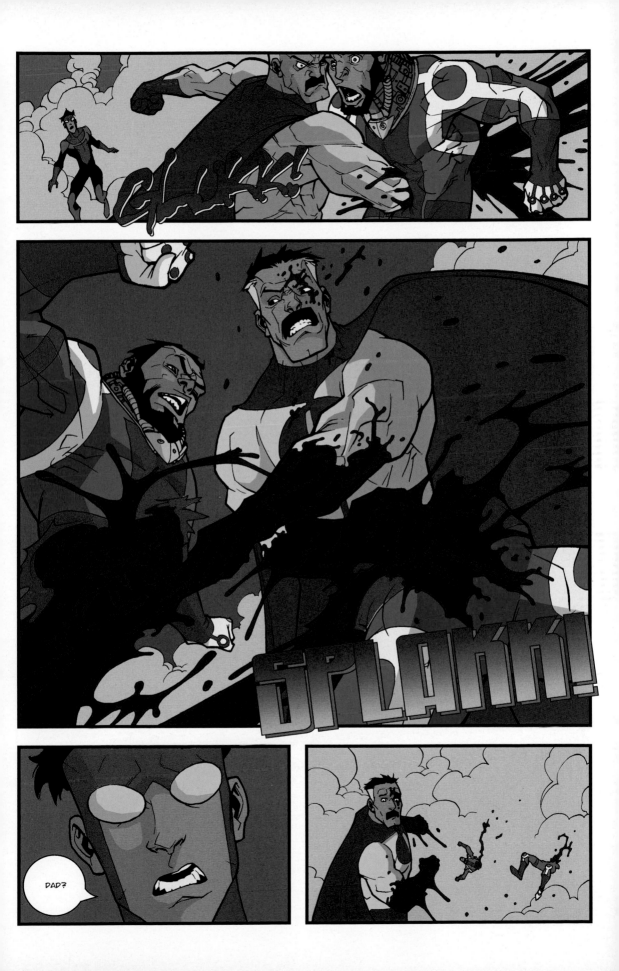

CHAPTER THREE

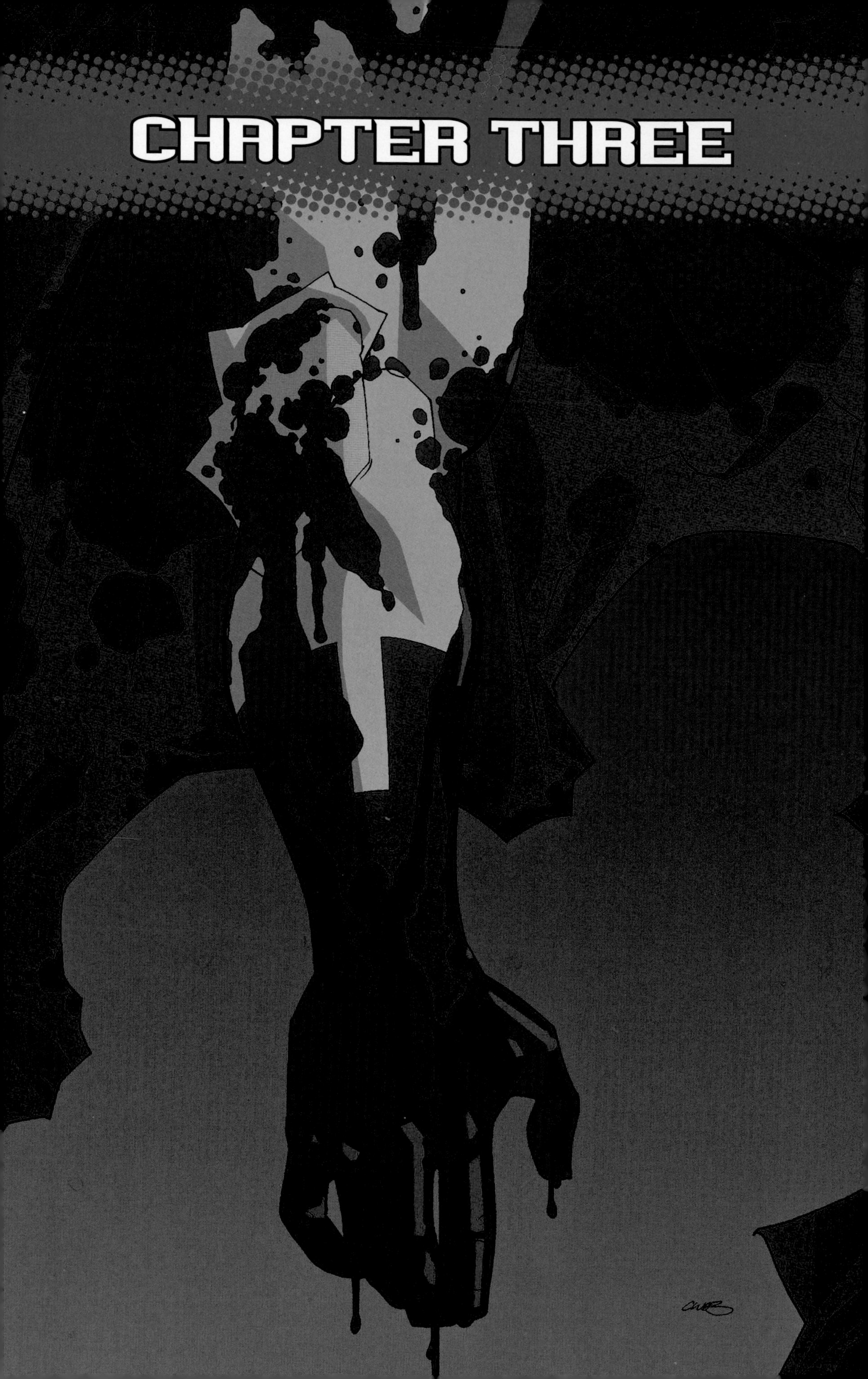

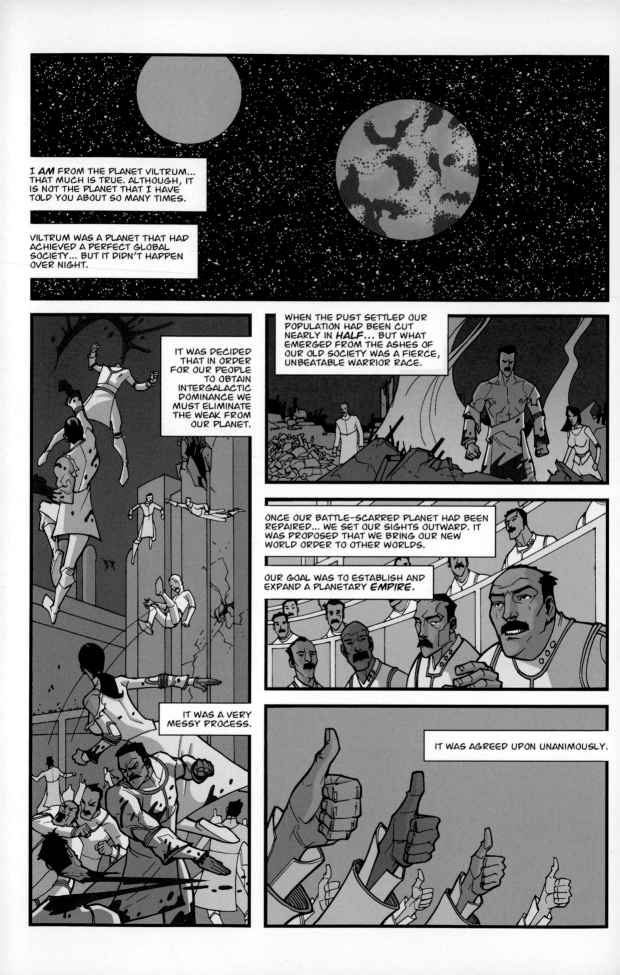

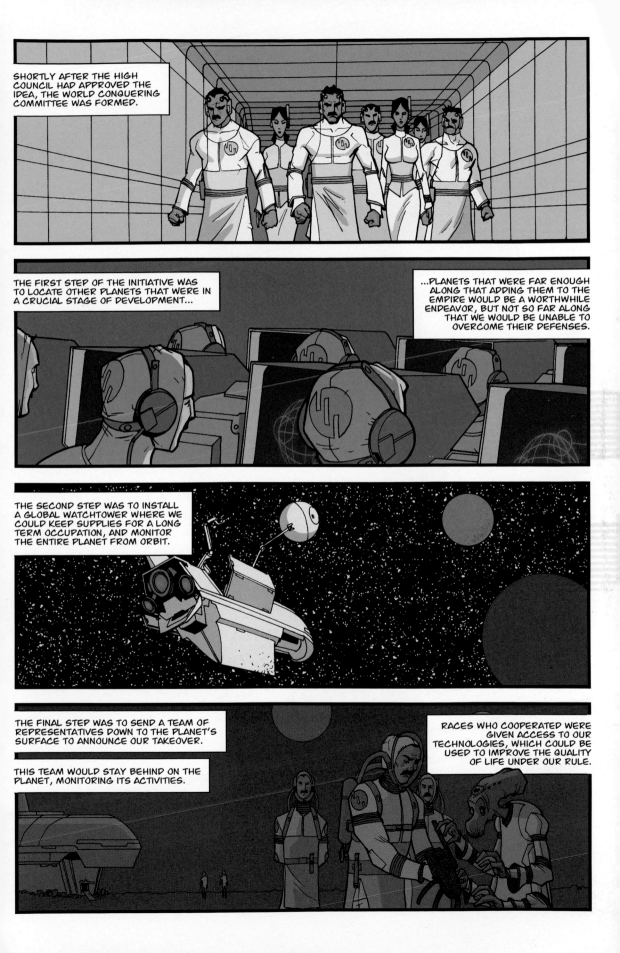

SHORTLY AFTER THE HIGH COUNCIL HAD APPROVED THE IDEA, THE WORLD CONQUERING COMMITTEE WAS FORMED.

THE FIRST STEP OF THE INITIATIVE WAS TO LOCATE OTHER PLANETS THAT WERE IN A CRUCIAL STAGE OF DEVELOPMENT...

...PLANETS THAT WERE FAR ENOUGH ALONG THAT ADDING THEM TO THE EMPIRE WOULD BE A WORTHWHILE ENDEAVOR, BUT NOT SO FAR ALONG THAT WE WOULD BE UNABLE TO OVERCOME THEIR DEFENSES.

THE SECOND STEP WAS TO INSTALL A GLOBAL WATCHTOWER WHERE WE COULD KEEP SUPPLIES FOR A LONG TERM OCCUPATION, AND MONITOR THE ENTIRE PLANET FROM ORBIT.

THE FINAL STEP WAS TO SEND A TEAM OF REPRESENTATIVES DOWN TO THE PLANET'S SURFACE TO ANNOUNCE OUR TAKEOVER.

THIS TEAM WOULD STAY BEHIND ON THE PLANET, MONITORING ITS ACTIVITIES.

RACES WHO COOPERATED WERE GIVEN ACCESS TO OUR TECHNOLOGIES, WHICH COULD BE USED TO IMPROVE THE QUALITY OF LIFE UNDER OUR RULE.

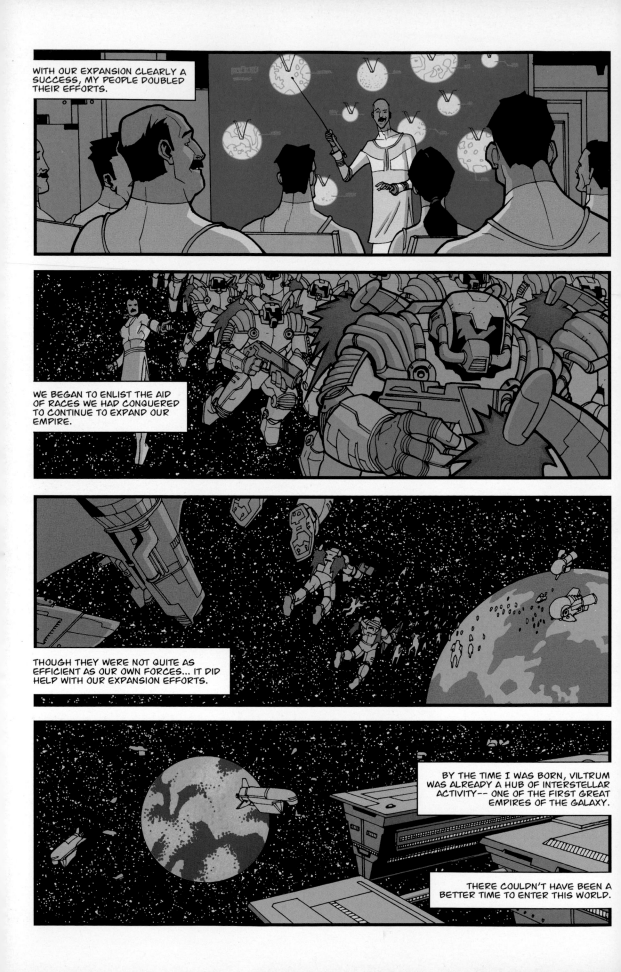

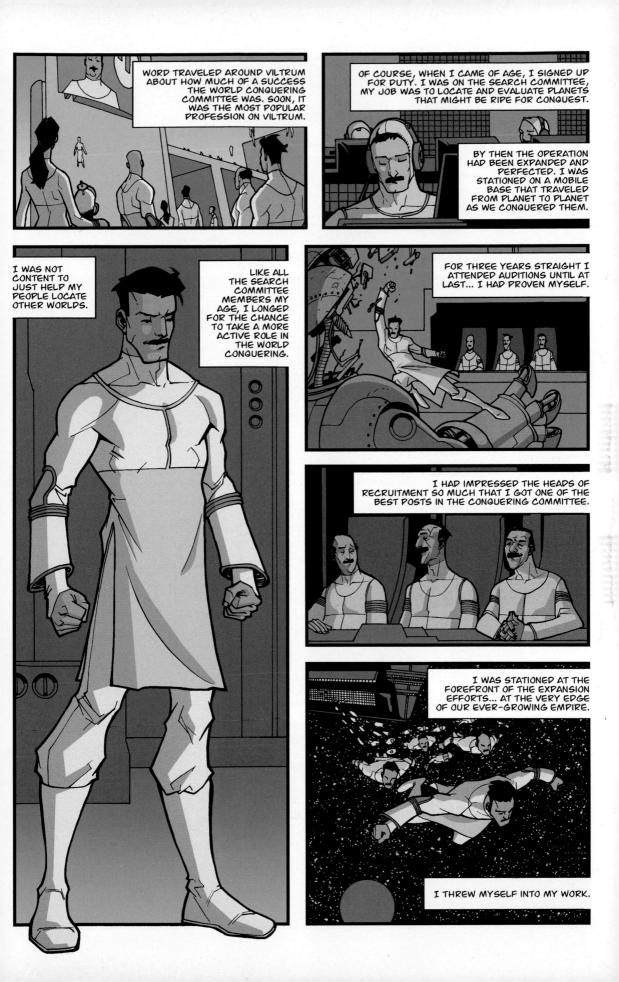

WORD TRAVELED AROUND VILTRUM ABOUT HOW MUCH OF A SUCCESS THE WORLD CONQUERING COMMITTEE WAS. SOON, IT WAS THE MOST POPULAR PROFESSION ON VILTRUM.

OF COURSE, WHEN I CAME OF AGE, I SIGNED UP FOR DUTY. I WAS ON THE SEARCH COMMITTEE, MY JOB WAS TO LOCATE AND EVALUATE PLANETS THAT MIGHT BE RIPE FOR CONQUEST.

BY THEN THE OPERATION HAD BEEN EXPANDED AND PERFECTED. I WAS STATIONED ON A MOBILE BASE THAT TRAVELED FROM PLANET TO PLANET AS WE CONQUERED THEM.

I WAS NOT CONTENT TO JUST HELP MY PEOPLE LOCATE OTHER WORLDS.

LIKE ALL THE SEARCH COMMITTEE MEMBERS MY AGE, I LONGED FOR THE CHANCE TO TAKE A MORE ACTIVE ROLE IN THE WORLD CONQUERING.

FOR THREE YEARS STRAIGHT I ATTENDED AUDITIONS UNTIL AT LAST... I HAD PROVEN MYSELF.

I HAD IMPRESSED THE HEADS OF RECRUITMENT SO MUCH THAT I GOT ONE OF THE BEST POSTS IN THE CONQUERING COMMITTEE.

I WAS STATIONED AT THE FOREFRONT OF THE EXPANSION EFFORTS... AT THE VERY EDGE OF OUR EVER-GROWING EMPIRE.

I THREW MYSELF INTO MY WORK.

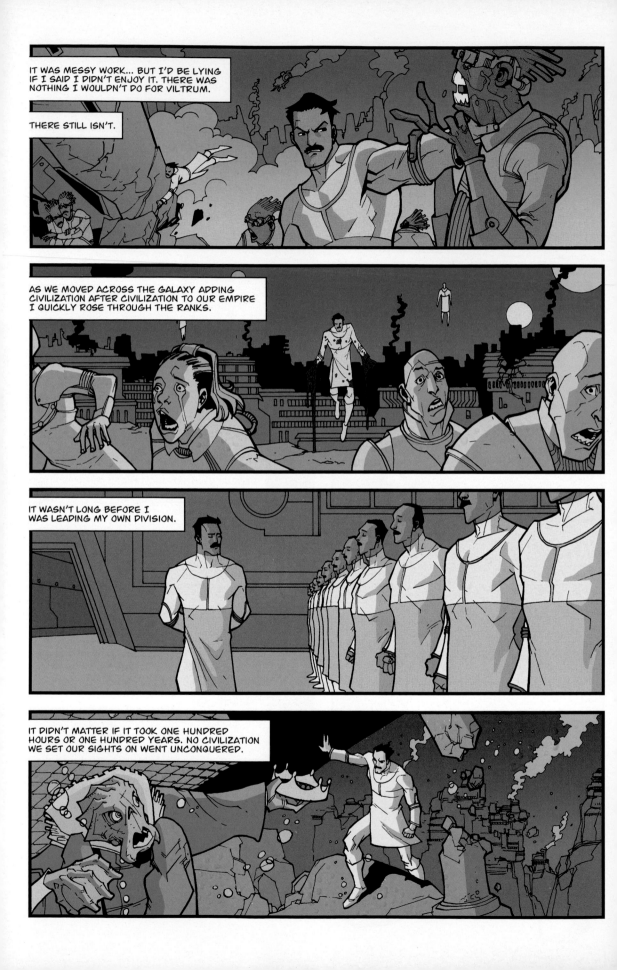

...AND EVENTUALLY... WITH MUCH MORE.

AS OUR EMPIRE GREW, OUR FORCES BECAME STRETCHED TOO THIN JUST TRYING TO MAINTAIN IT.

OUR EXPANSION SCREECHED TO AN ABRUPT HALT.

IT WAS CLEAR THAT WE NEEDED A MORE EFFICIENT METHOD OF WORLD CONQUERING.

SO ONE WAS DEVISED.

RATHER THAN COME IN LARGE NUMBERS AND CONQUER A PLANET BY FORCE, OUR HIGHEST RANKED AND MOST TRUSTED OFFICERS WOULD BE ESSENTIALLY GIVEN PLANETS TO SURVEY AND WEAKEN OVER TIME.

I WAS ONE OF THE FIRST CHOSEN FOR THIS ASSIGNMENT.

WE WERE TO ACCLIMATE OURSELVES WITH THE PLANET'S ENVIRONMENT... EVENTUALLY BECOMING A MEMBER OF SOCIETY.

ASIDE FROM ENSURING THE PLANET DID NOT BECOME STRONG ENOUGH TO DEFEND ITSELF FROM US, IT WOULD BE OURS TO DO WITH AS WE PLEASED FOR FIVE HUNDRED YEARS.

AT THE END OF THAT TIME, THE KNOWLEDGE WE HAD COLLECTED WOULD BE USED TO QUICKLY AND EFFICIENTLY BRING THE PLANET UNDER VILTRUM RULE.

IT WAS A PRIVILEGE TO BE GIVEN THIS ASSIGNMENT-- A REWARD FOR ALL MY HARD WORK.

IT WAS THE CLOSEST THING TO A VACATION THAT EXISTED ON VILTRUM.

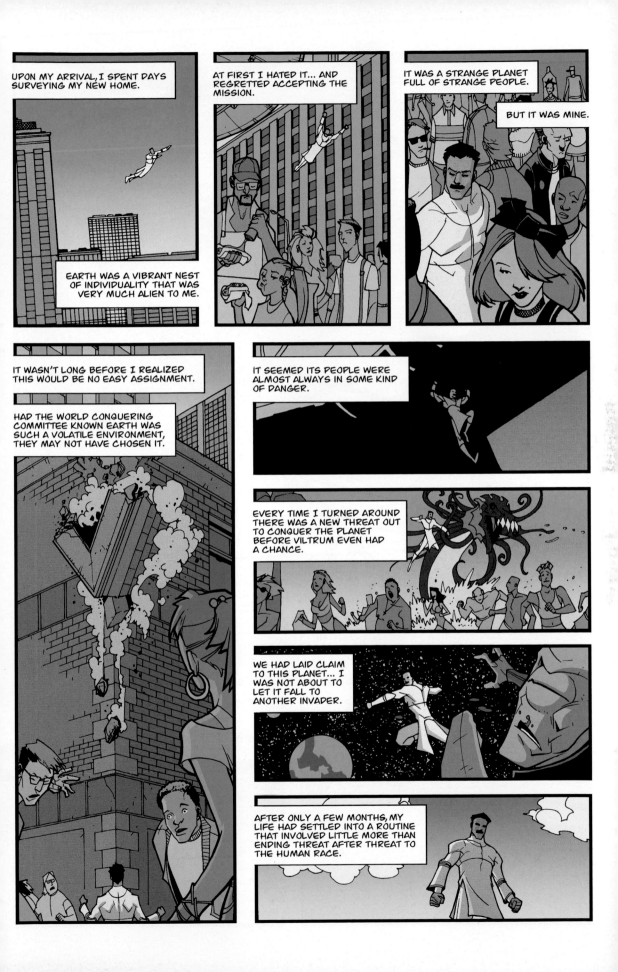

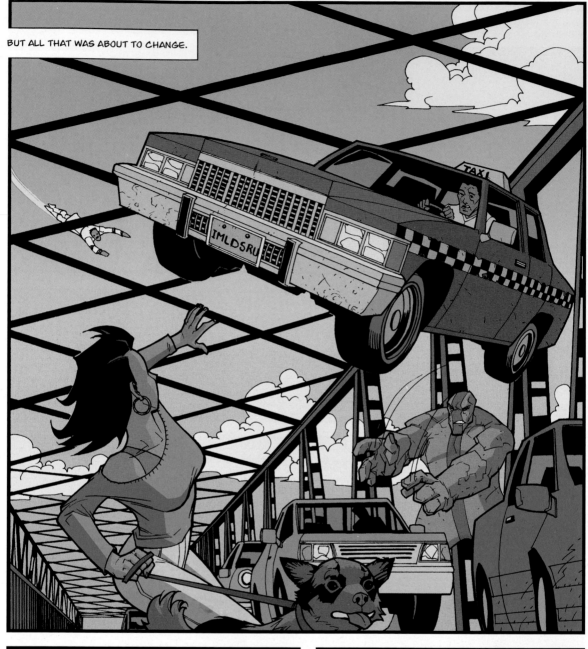

BUT ALL THAT WAS ABOUT TO CHANGE.

WHEN I MET YOUR MOTHER I KNEW THE ONLY WAY TO ENJOY MY TIME HERE WAS TO ACTUALLY LIVE AS A HUMAN.

WHEN IT EVENTUALLY CAME UP... I TOLD HER THE VERSION OF MY COMING TO EARTH THAT YOU HAVE BEEN TOLD SINCE CHILDHOOD.

IT WAS CLEAR SHE WOULDN'T APPROVE OF THE REAL REASONS I WAS HERE.

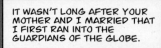

IT WASN'T LONG AFTER YOUR MOTHER AND I MARRIED THAT I FIRST RAN INTO THE GUARDIANS OF THE GLOBE.

I NEVER BECAME AN **OFFICIAL** MEMBER BUT I WAS WELCOMED INTO THE FOLD WITH OPEN ARMS.

THEY HELPED ME ALONG IN THE EARLY YEARS. THEY KNEW I WAS NEW TO ALL THIS AND WERE ALL TOO EAGER TO ASSIST ME.

SOME OF THEM I WOULD EVEN EVENTUALLY COME TO CONSIDER FRIENDS.

BUT I KNEW THEY WOULD NEVER ALLOW ME TO COMPLETE MY MISSION.

I KNEW THAT THEY WOULD EVENTUALLY NEED TO BE **ELIMINATED.**

I DECIDED THAT FOR A TIME I WOULD TURN MY BACK ON MY DUTIES AND FOCUS ON RAISING YOU.

I THOUGHT THAT YOU WOULD BE ABLE TO PROVIDE A UNIQUE PERSPECTIVE TO THE WORLD CONQUERING COMMITTEE, HAVING GROWN UP IN THIS ALIEN ENVIRONMENT.

HONESTLY, I WAS HAPPY IN MY NEW LIFE... BUT I KNEW IT COULDN'T LAST.

WHEN YOU STARTED TO DEVELOP YOUR POWERS... I KNEW I COULDN'T WAIT MUCH LONGER.

SO I MADE THE FIRST STEP TOWARDS WEAKENING EARTH'S DEFENSES.

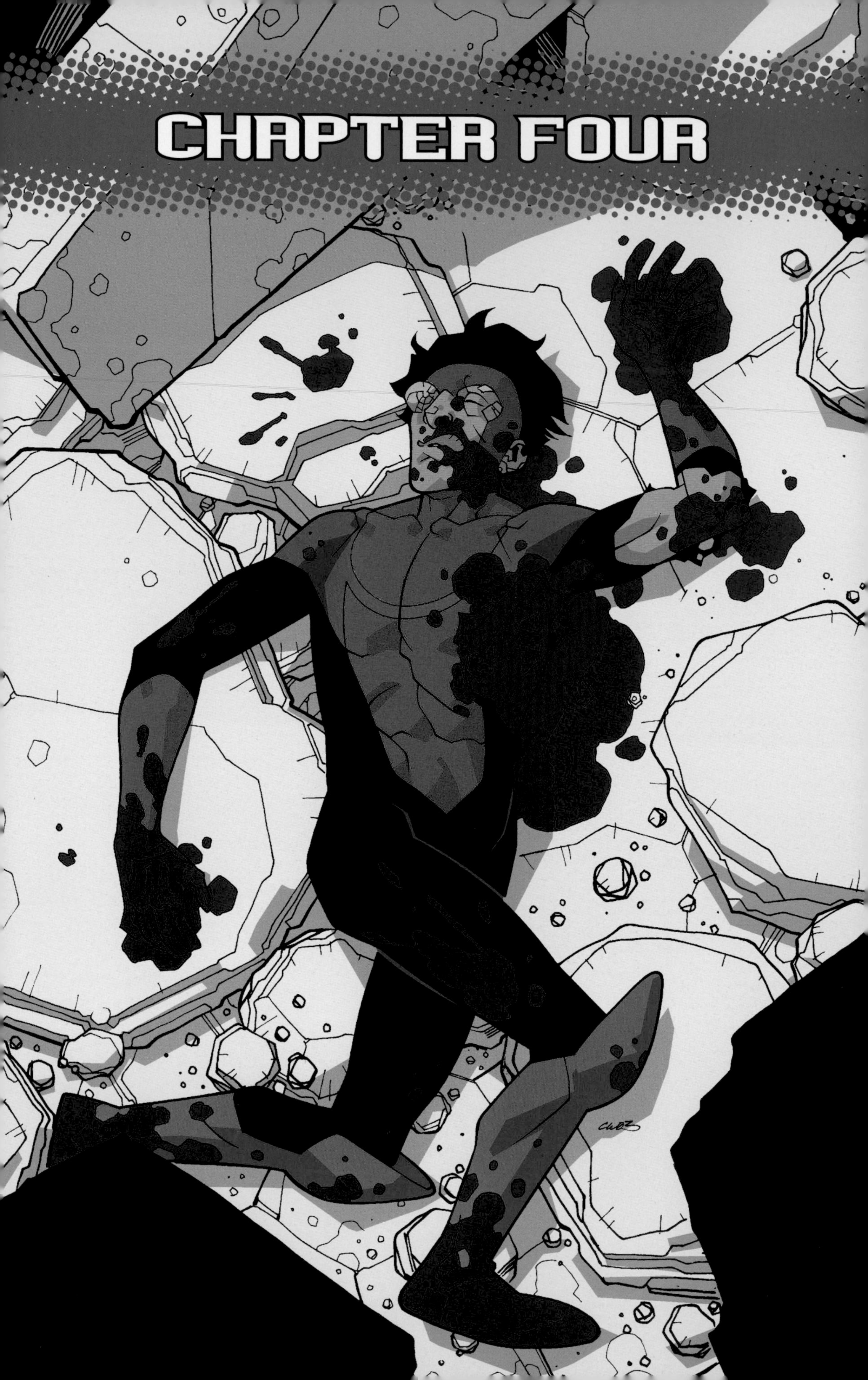
CHAPTER FOUR

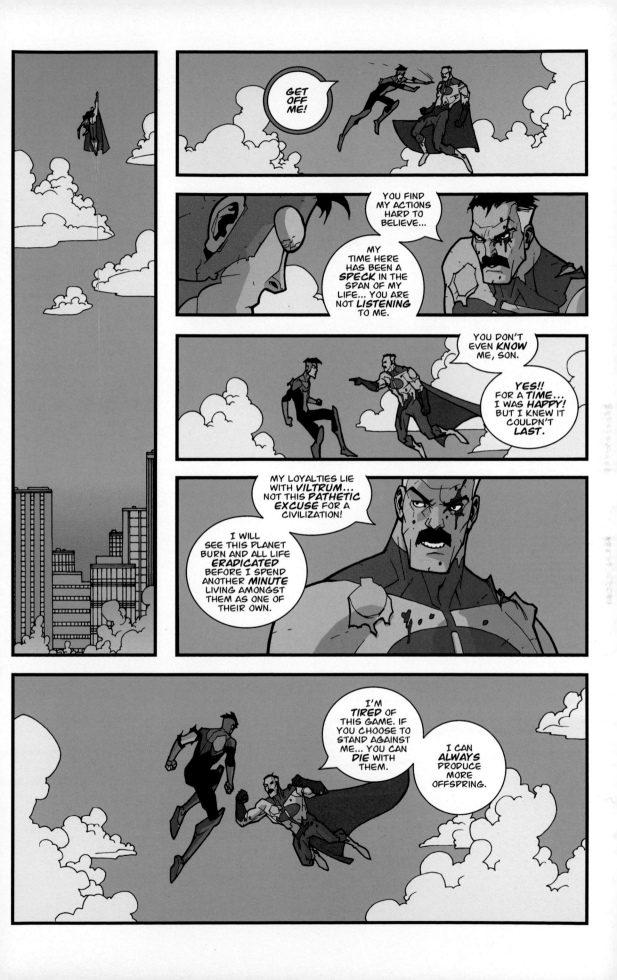

SPLOOSH!

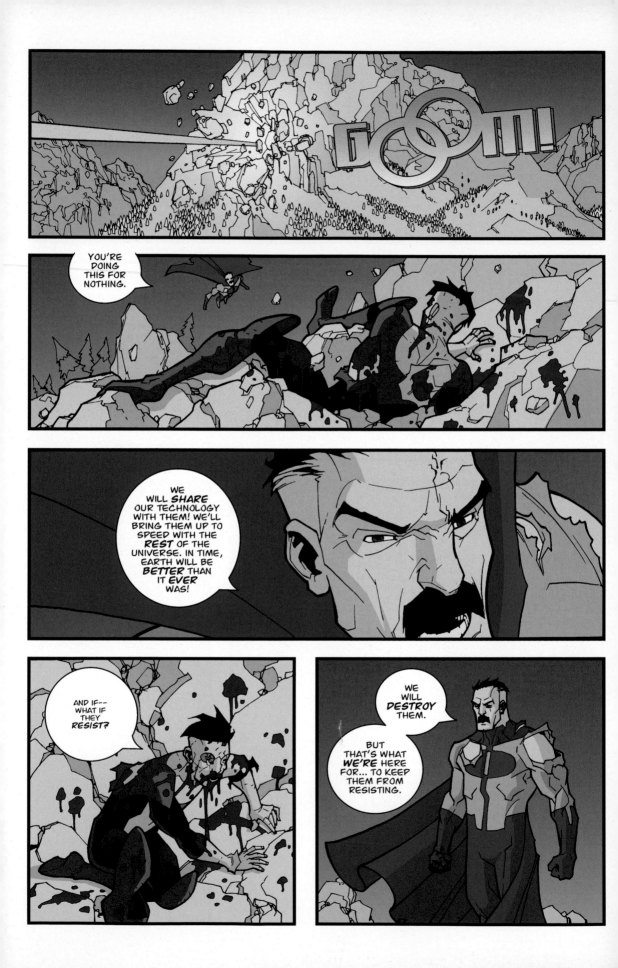

YOU DAD.

I'D STILL HAVE YOU.

...

DAD?

CHAPTER FIVE

HUH?

OH, *GOOD*... YOU'RE AWAKE.

I--

I THOUGHT IT MIGHT HAVE BEEN A DREAM...

BELIEVE ME, KID. I WISH IT *WERE*.

YOU'VE BEEN OUT FOR ALMOST *TWO WEEKS*... BUT MY GUYS HAVE GOT YOU PATCHED UP REAL GOOD.

YOU SHOULD BE BACK UP TO FULL SPEED IN A DAY OR TWO. WE'RE BASICALLY JUST KEEPING YOU HERE FOR OBSERVATION. WE WANT TO MAKE SURE THERE'S NOTHING WRONG THAT WE MISSED.

OH... HEY, WILLIAM.

OH-- UM-- HEY.

UH.

HAVE YOU HEARD FROM *MARK?* HE HASN'T BEEN IN SCHOOL FOR *TWO WEEKS* AND I'M STARTING TO GET *WORRIED.*

NO. NOBODY IS AT HOME AND I HAVEN'T HEARD FROM HIM SINCE THAT STUFF BETWEEN HIS FATHER AND HIM WAS ON THE *NEWS.*

I'M REALLY, UH--

WAIT A MINUTE! YOU *KNOW?*

OH, MAN... YOU KNOW *TOO?!* THANK *GOD!* I THOUGHT I TOTALLY *BLEW* IT.

SO, YOU THINK HE'S OKAY?

I DON'T KNOW.

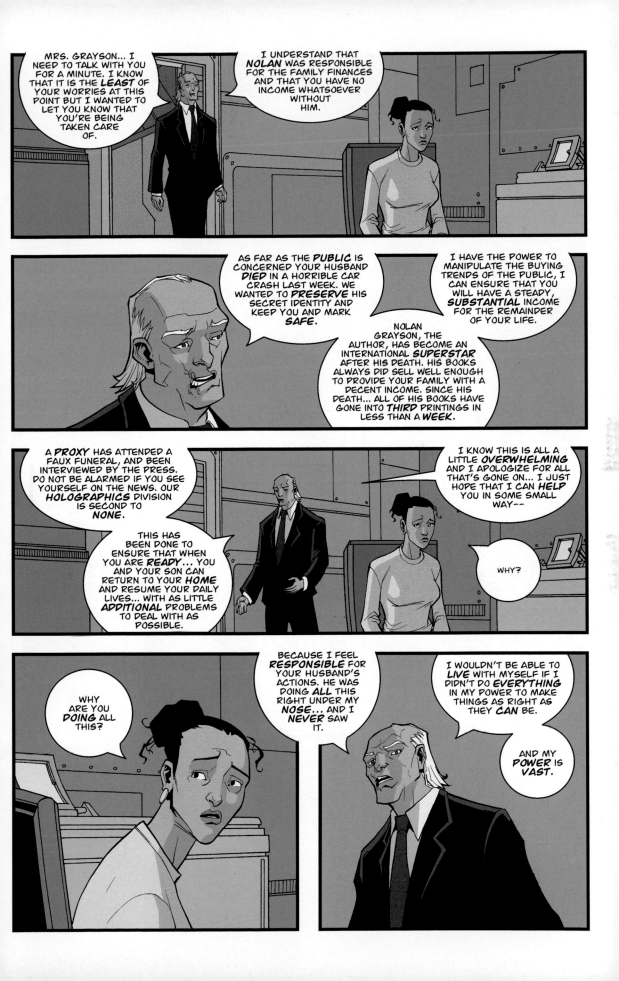

UNITED STATES
PENTAGON

Parking in Rear

THANKS FOR WAITING. SORRY FOR THE DELAY.

NO PROBLEM AT ALL, DONALD.

BEFORE WE START THE MEETING, IT'S BEEN BROUGHT TO MY ATTENTION THAT A COLLEAGUE OF MINE HAS GONE *MISSING*. INVINCIBLE HASN'T BEEN SEEN OR HEARD FROM SINCE THE INCIDENT WITH HIS FATHER, OMNI-MAN, WAS ALL OVER THE NEWS.

I WAS WONDERING IF YOU'D BE *WILLING* TO ALLOW ME TO--

HE'S *FINE.* WE HAVE HIM IN CUSTODY. HE WAS INJURED AND WE HAVE BEEN PROVIDING HIM WITH MEDICAL ATTENTION. BUT ROBOT, BETWEEN YOU AND I... HE'S THE *LEAST* OF YOUR CONCERNS.

YOUR HANDPICKED *GUARDIANS OF THE GLOBE* ARE STRUGGLING. THE RESPONSE TIME OF YOUR TEAM LEAVES *MUCH* TO BE DESIRED AND WHILE YOU HAVEN'T OUTRIGHT *FAILED* ON A MISSION YET... THE TOP BRASS IS *NOT* HAPPY.

ALL EYES ARE ON *YOU.* YOU NEED TO MAKE SURE YOU DON'T MESS ANYTHING UP IN THE COMING WEEKS. YOU'RE MORE OR LESS ON *PROBATION.*

I SEE.

UNDERSTOOD.

I TURNED THE LIGHTS OFF FOR A **SECOND** JUST SO YOU COULD SEE WHAT I'M TALKING ABOUT. I HOPE YOU DIDN'T SEE **TOO** MUCH... IF YOU DID... I'LL HAVE TO **KILL** YOU.

HAH **HAH!** VERY FUNNY.

AN OLDIE BUT A GOODIE.

SO IF IT'S THE **LIGHT** IN THE ROOM THAT'S MAKING ME UNABLE TO **SEE** ANYTHING, HOW COME I CAN SEE **MYSELF**... AND **YOU?**

THAT'S... COMPLICATED.

WE DIDN'T WANT YOU TO BE **TOO** ALARMED WHEN YOU CAME IN... IT WAS IMPORTANT THAT YOU AT LEAST SEE **SOMETHING.**

EXPLAINING THAT WOULD BE A WASTE OF TIME... A **LOT** OF TIME.

WE HAVE **PROOF** THAT THERE **ARE** OTHER PLANETS CAPABLE OF SUPPORTING LIFE. KNOWING HOW **LONG** HE CAN HOLD HIS BREATH AND HOW **FAST** HE CAN FLY... IT IS NOT **UNREASONABLE** TO ASSUME YOUR FATHER COULD MAKE IT TO ONE OF THESE PLANETS.

HE WAS **NOT** COMMITTING SUICIDE BY FLYING INTO SPACE--THAT WAS ONE OF OUR TECHNICIANS' THEORIES--AT LEAST... WE'RE PRETTY SURE HE WASN'T.

WHAT I'M GETTING AT IS HE'S **GONE.** YOUR FATHER WAS VERY VALUABLE TO US... ESPECIALLY AFTER THE GUARDIANS OF THE GLOBE WERE DEAD. HE SAVED A LOT OF LIVES AND THIS ENTIRE PLANET MORE TIMES THAN I CAN REMEMBER.

WE NEED A REPLACEMENT.

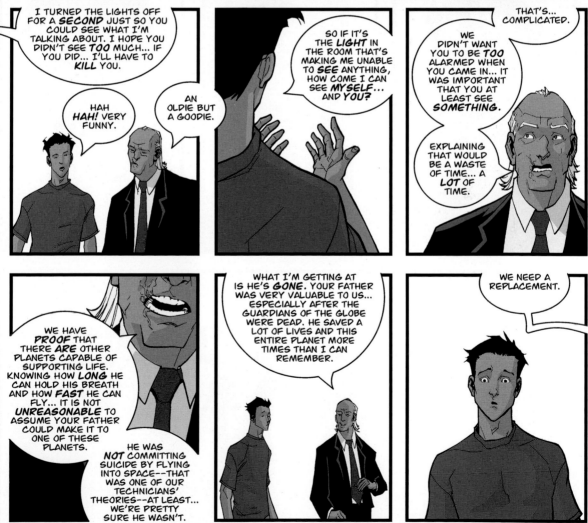

EVE?

OH, GOOD. I WAS AFRAID YOUR PARENTS WOULD ANSWER THE DOOR. I HADN'T COME UP WITH A GOOD **EXCUSE** FOR BEING HERE THAT DIDN'T INVOLVE OUR MUTUAL FRIEND BEING A SUPERHERO.

WHAT CAN I DO FOR YOU? DID YOU HEAR FROM MARK?

NO, BUT MY... UM... **FRIEND**... WORKS FOR THE GOVERNMENT, AND HE SAYS THAT HE WAS INJURED... BUT THAT THEY HAVE HIM AND HE'S HEALING UP.

HE SHOULD BE BACK SOON.

SO MARK'S FINE? **GOOD.** THAT'S GREAT NEWS. MAN, I WAS **SO** WORRIED ABOUT HIM.

ME **TOO.**

BUT HE'S **SAFE** NOW.

...

YOU WANT TO GET SOMETHING TO **EAT**... TO CELEBRATE?

...

SO...

I'M GOING TO BED.

MOM... ARE YOU *OKAY?*

NO. NOT EVEN *CLOSE.*

SO... *YOU'RE* A VILTRUMITE?

BUT YOU DON'T *WORK* FOR THEM... AND YOUR DAD *LEFT*. HE JUST *LEFT*.

YEAH. I'VE NEVER EVEN *BEEN* TO VILTRUM. I DON'T REALLY KNOW MUCH ABOUT THEM. BUT *YEAH*... AS FAR AS WE CAN TELL MY DAD IS JUST *GONE*.

THAT IS *HIGHLY* UNORTHODOX BEHAVIOR FOR A VILTRUMITE. THEY DON'T JUST *LEAVE* THEIR POST. THEY DESTROYED MY HOME WORLD HUNDREDS OF YEARS AGO. MY PEOPLE ARE A NOMADIC SPECIES BECAUSE WE *RESISTED* THE VILTRUMITES WHEN THEY ATTEMPTED TO TAKE OVER.

I'M VERY SORRY.

DON'T BE. YOU HAD NO PART IN IT... FROM THE SOUNDS OF IT... *I'M* THE ONE THAT SHOULD BE APOLOGIZING TO *YOU*. IF I HAD CHECKED MY RECORDS *BEFORE* I LEFT HERE, I MIGHT HAVE SEEN THAT EARTH HAD BEEN FLAGGED AS BEING PREPPED FOR A VILTRUMITE TAKEOVER.

I COULD HAVE *WARNED* YOU.

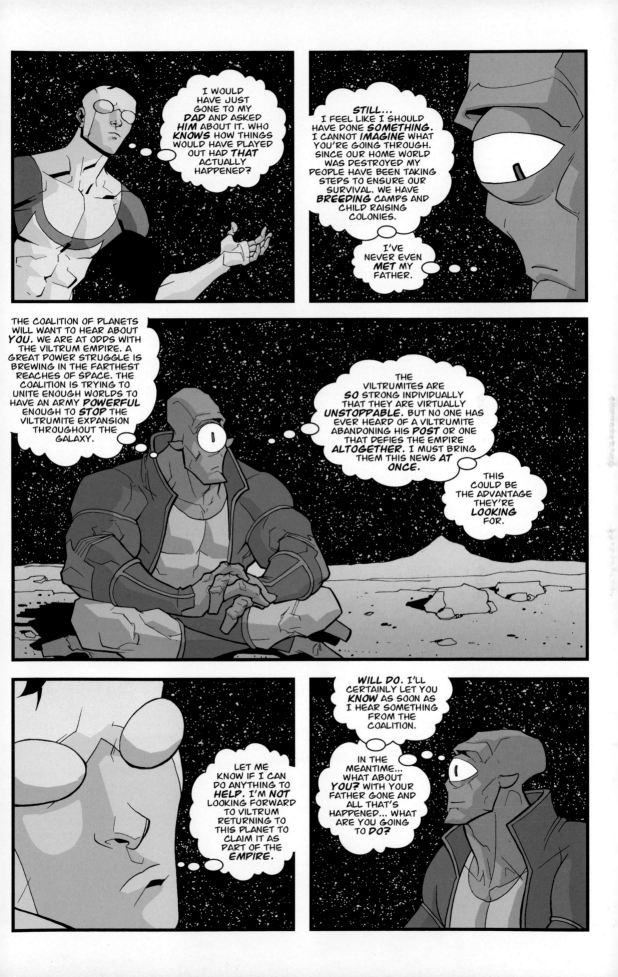

As with all our trades we've had two versions of the cover. To your right there you should see the original version of the cover to this book. Above we have some of Cory's sketches for the cover. We did new covers for the second printings of the first two volumes. They are both pretty cool and both featured some kind of panel layout behind a central figure featuring side characters in the book. I don't like having multiple covers on the same book but I LIKED the panel design enough to make it the standard for our TPB covers. So instead of adding panels to a new cover when we do the eventual second printing of this book, I asked Cory to add some panels behind this cover. Instead... he decided to redraw the whole thing. You should have seen the look on Bill's face when he found out he got to color this cover all over again.

Here we have some sketches for the new version of the cover to this collection. Have I mentioned how much I love Donald? Man, that dude is so cool. Cecil Stedman is a character I've always planned on bringing into the book after Nolan did his thing in this arc. For kick, I thought it would be fun to introduce him in Brit instead of this book. That way he would seem established when he showed up here. Donald however was brought over from Brit because I love him as much as a heterosexual writer can love a fictional man. Don't believe me? Read the third Brit one-shot. I had to stop doing those because the forth one was going to be called "Brit: Really Donald's Book."

Here we see some of Cory's sketches for the covers of the issues collected in this volume.

Ah, now that we've got Cory out of the way I can go into detail about how much I love Ryan Ottley (almost as much as Donald). Ryan really pulled this book's fat out of the fire. Once Cory realized the monthly grind was not his thing, Ryan was brought in to take over this book. He really hit the ground running, pumping out the issues contained in this trade at what seemed like an alarming rate but what in reality turned out to be... a monthly schedule. With this book back on track, sales started climbing and rather than worrying if I was going to have to end the series at issue 13, I got to start thinking about how I was going to get to what I had planned for issue 15. Ryan Ottley saved this book. Aside from being a timely fellow, Ryan is also mighty talented, more so actually. On top of that the man is improving at an alarming rate. Comparing issue 9 to issue 13 in this book is like comparing night to day. Ryan has really taken this book and made it his own and I couldn't be happier to have him.

Oh... the art. Um... Ryan gets asked to do commission drawing all the time. I run them as pin-ups in the book. So this page and the next has all his commission drawings on it. Woo!

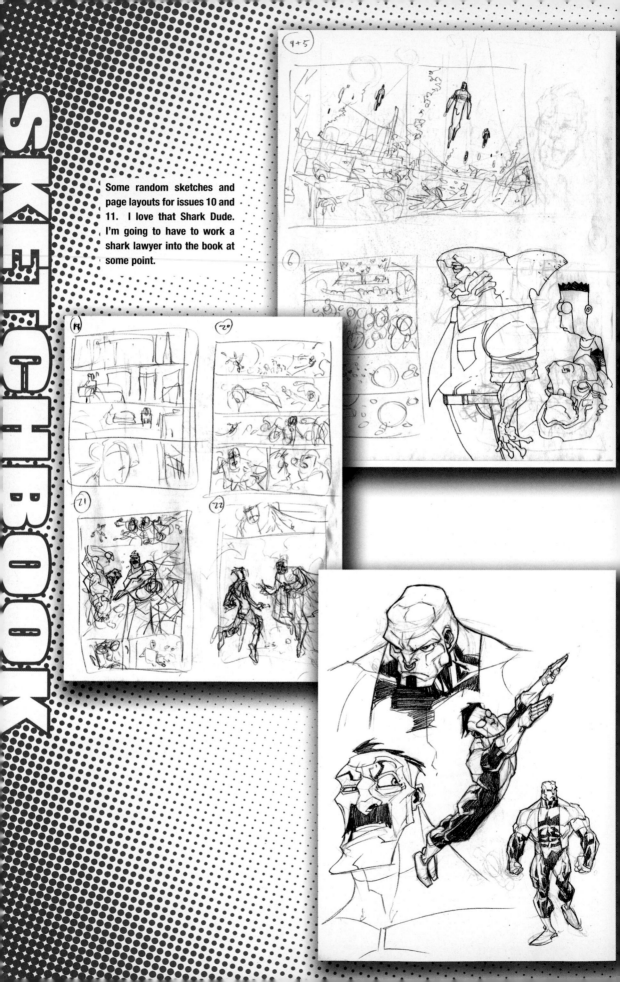

SKETCHBOOK

Some random sketches and page layouts for issues 10 and 11. I love that Shark Dude. I'm going to have to work a shark lawyer into the book at some point.

More page layouts and sketches and some alien designs by Ryan. 11 was a tough one for ol' Ryan. He had to come up with loads of alien designs and cities and stuff just on the fly. There was a ton of stuff to reference too, aside from just making some of the panels match the pages from issue 2 that Cory did. Ryan's always been a real trooper when I ask him to swipe stuff. He's very much against it but I think it's important to the story to show artistically how the events paralleled to the original origin Nolan told in issue 2... so I make him do it. What a trooper.

WATCHOO LOOKINAT PUNK ?!?

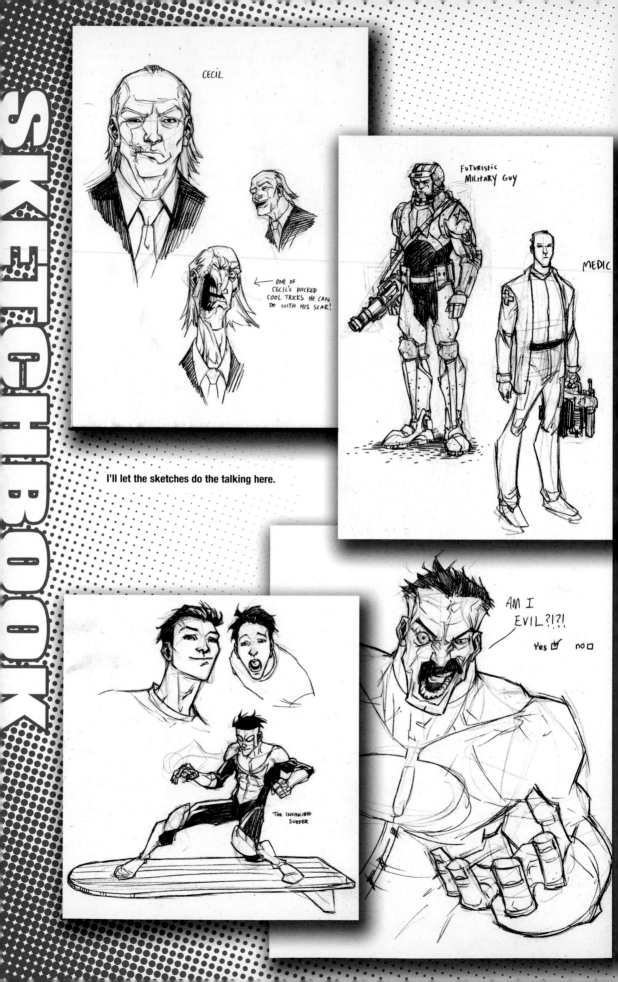

I'll let the sketches do the talking here.